This journal belongs to:

_____

Project name: _____

Who I'm making it for: _____

Occasion: _____

Start date: _____ End date: _____

Sketch

Notes:

_____

_____

_____

_____

_____

_____

Yarn used

Color: _____

Dye lot: _____

Fiber: _____

Guage: _____

Weight: _____

WPI: _____

Hooks used: _____

Washing instructions: _____

_____

_____

Additional notes:

_____

_____

_____

_____

_____

_____

Project name: _____

Who I'm making it for: _____

Occasion: _____

Start date: _____ End date: _____

Sketch

Notes:

_____

_____

_____

_____

_____

_____

_____

Yarn used

Color: _____

Dye lot: _____

Fiber: _____

Guage: _____

Weight: _____

WPI: _____

Hooks used: _____

Washing instructions: _____
_____
_____

Additional notes:
_____
_____
_____
_____
_____
_____

Project name: _____

Who I'm making it for: _____

Occasion: _____

Start date: _____ End date: _____

Sketch

Notes:

_____

_____

_____

_____

_____

_____

_____

Yarn used

Color: _____

Dye lot: _____

Fiber: _____

Guage:_____

Weight: _____

WPI: _____

Hooks used:_____

Washing instructions:_____

_____

_____

Additional notes:

_____

_____

_____

_____

_____

_____

Project name: _____

Who I'm making it for: _____

Occasion: _____

Start date: _____ End date: _____

Sketch

Notes:

_____

_____

_____

_____

_____

_____

_____

Yarn used

Color: _____

Dye lot: _____

Fiber: _____

Guage: _____

Weight: _____

WPI: _____

Hooks used: _____

Washing instructions: _____
_____
_____

Additional notes:
_____
_____
_____
_____
_____
_____

Project name: _____

Who I'm making it for: _____

Occasion: _____

Start date: _____ End date: _____

Sketch

Notes:

_____

_____

_____

_____

_____

_____

_____

Yarn used

Color: _____

Dye lot: _____

Fiber: _____

Guage: _____

Weight: _____

WPI: _____

Hooks used: _____

Washing instructions: _____

_____

_____

Additional notes:

_____

_____

_____

_____

_____

_____

Project name: _____

Who I'm making it for: _____

Occasion: _____

Start date: _____ End date: _____

Sketch

Notes:

_____

_____

_____

_____

_____

_____

_____

Yarn used

Color: _____

Dye lot: _____

Fiber: _____

Guage: _____

Weight: _____

WPI: _____

Hooks used: _____

Washing instructions: _____

_____

_____

Additional notes:

_____

_____

_____

_____

_____

_____

Project name: _____

Who I'm making it for: _____

Occasion: _____

Start date: _____ End date: _____

Sketch

Notes:

_____

_____

_____

_____

_____

_____

_____

Yarn used

Color: _____

Dye lot: _____

Fiber: _____

Guage: _____

Weight: _____

WPI: _____

Hooks used: _____

Washing instructions: _____

_____

_____

Additional notes:

_____

_____

_____

_____

_____

_____

_____

Project name: _____

Who I'm making it for: _____

Occasion: _____

Start date: _____ End date: _____

Sketch

Notes:

_____

_____

_____

_____

_____

_____

_____

Yarn used

Color: _____

Dye lot: _____

Fiber: _____

Guage: _____

Weight: _____

WPI: _____

Hooks used: _____

Washing instructions: _____

_____

_____

Additional notes:

_____

_____

_____

_____

_____

_____

Project name: _____

Who I'm making it for: _____

Occasion: _____

Start date: _____ End date: _____

Sketch

Notes:

_____

_____

_____

_____

_____

_____

_____

Yarn used

Color: _____

Dye lot: _____

Fiber: _____

Guage: _____

Weight: _____

WPI: _____

Hooks used: _____

Washing instructions: _____

_____

_____

Additional notes:

_____

_____

_____

_____

_____

_____

Project name: _____

Who I'm making it for: _____

Occasion: _____

Start date: _____ End date: _____

Sketch

Notes:

_____

_____

_____

_____

_____

_____

_____

Yarn used

Color: _____

Dye lot: _____

Fiber: _____

Guage: _____

Weight: _____

WPI: _____

Hooks used: _____

Washing instructions: _____

_____

_____

Additional notes:

_____

_____

_____

_____

_____

_____

Project name: _____

Who I'm making it for: _____

Occasion: _____

Start date: _____ End date: _____

Sketch

Notes:

_____

_____

_____

_____

_____

_____

_____

Yarn used

Color: _____

Dye lot: _____

Fiber: _____

Guage: _____

Weight: _____

WPI: _____

Hooks used: _____

Washing instructions: _____

_____

_____

Additional notes:

_____

_____

_____

_____

_____

_____

_____

Project name: _____

Who I'm making it for: _____

Occasion: _____

Start date: _____ End date: _____

Sketch

Notes:

_____

_____

_____

_____

_____

_____

_____

Yarn used

Color: _____

Dye lot: _____

Fiber: _____

Guage: _____

Weight: _____

WPI: _____

Hooks used: _____

Washing instructions: _____

_____

_____

Additional notes:

_____

_____

_____

_____

_____

_____

Project name: _____

Who I'm making it for: _____

Occasion: _____

Start date: _____ End date: _____

Sketch

Notes:

_____

_____

_____

_____

_____

_____

Yarn used

Color: _____

Dye lot: _____

Fiber: _____

Guage: _____

Weight: _____

WPI: _____

Hooks used: _____

Washing instructions: _____

_____

_____

Additional notes:

_____

_____

_____

_____

_____

_____

Project name: _____

Who I'm making it for: _____

Occasion: _____

Start date: _____ End date: _____

Sketch

Notes:

_____

_____

_____

_____

_____

_____

_____

Yarn used

Color: _____

Dye lot: _____

Fiber: _____

Guage: _____

Weight: _____

WPI: _____

Hooks used: _____

Washing instructions: _____

_____

_____

Additional notes:

_____

_____

_____

_____

_____

_____

Project name: _____

Who I'm making it for: _____

Occasion: _____

Start date: _____ End date: _____

Sketch

Notes:

_____

_____

_____

_____

_____

_____

_____

Yarn used

Color: _____

Dye lot: _____

Fiber: _____

Guage: _____

Weight: _____

WPI: _____

Hooks used: _____

Washing instructions: _____

_____

_____

Additional notes:

_____

_____

_____

_____

_____

_____

Project name: _____

Who I'm making it for: _____

Occasion: _____

Start date: _____ End date: _____

Sketch

Notes:

_____

_____

_____

_____

_____

_____

Yarn used

Color: _____

Dye lot: _____

Fiber: _____

Guage: _____

Weight: _____

WPI: _____

Hooks used: _____

Washing instructions: _____

_____

_____

Additional notes:

_____

_____

_____

_____

_____

_____

Project name: _____

Who I'm making it for: _____

Occasion: _____

Start date: _____ End date: _____

Sketch

Notes:

_____

_____

_____

_____

_____

_____

_____

Yarn used

Color: _____

Dye lot: _____

Fiber: _____

Guage: _____

Weight: _____

WPI: _____

Hooks used: _____

Washing instructions: _____

_____

_____

Additional notes:

_____

_____

_____

_____

_____

_____

Project name: _____

Who I'm making it for: _____

Occasion: _____

Start date: _____ End date: _____

Sketch

Notes:

_____

_____

_____

_____

_____

_____

_____

Yarn used

Color: _____

Dye lot: _____

Fiber: _____

Guage: _____

Weight: _____

WPI: _____

Hooks used: _____

Washing instructions: _____

_____

_____

Additional notes:

_____

_____

_____

_____

_____

_____

Project name: _____

Who I'm making it for: _____

Occasion: _____

Start date: _____ End date: _____

Sketch

Notes:

_____

_____

_____

_____

_____

_____

Yarn used

Color: _____

Dye lot: _____

Fiber: _____

Guage:_____

Weight: _____

WPI: _____

Hooks used:_____

Washing instructions:_____

_____

_____

Additional notes:

_____

_____

_____

_____

_____

_____

Project name: _____

Who I'm making it for: _____

Occasion: _____

Start date: _____ End date: _____

Sketch

Notes:

_____

_____

_____

_____

_____

_____

_____

Yarn used

Color: _____

Dye lot: _____

Fiber: _____

Guage: _____

Weight: _____

WPI: _____

Hooks used: _____

Washing instructions: _____

_____

_____

Additional notes:

_____

_____

_____

_____

_____

_____

Project name: _____

Who I'm making it for: _____

Occasion: _____

Start date: _____ End date: _____

Sketch

Notes:

_____

_____

_____

_____

_____

_____

Yarn used

Color: _____

Dye lot: _____

Fiber: _____

Guage: _____

Weight: _____

WPI: _____

Hooks used: _____

Washing instructions: _____

_____

_____

Additional notes:

_____

_____

_____

_____

_____

_____

Project name: _____

Who I'm making it for: _____

Occasion: _____

Start date: _____ End date: _____

Sketch

Notes:

_____

_____

_____

_____

_____

_____

_____

Yarn used

Color: _____

Dye lot: _____

Fiber: _____

Guage:_____

Weight: _____

WPI: _____

Hooks used:_____

Washing instructions: _____

_____

_____

Additional notes:

_____

_____

_____

_____

_____

_____

Project name: _____

Who I'm making it for: _____

Occasion: _____

Start date: _____ End date: _____

Sketch

Notes:

_____

_____

_____

_____

_____

_____

_____

Yarn used

Color: _____

Dye lot: _____

Fiber: _____

Guage: _____

Weight: _____

WPI: _____

Hooks used: _____

Washing instructions: _____

_____

_____

Additional notes:

_____

_____

_____

_____

_____

_____

Project name: _____

Who I'm making it for: _____

Occasion: _____

Start date: _____ End date: _____

Sketch

Notes:

_____

_____

_____

_____

_____

_____

_____

Yarn used

Color: _____

Dye lot: _____

Fiber: _____

Guage: _____

Weight: _____

WPI: _____

Hooks used: _____

Washing instructions: _____

_____

_____

Additional notes:

_____

_____

_____

_____

_____

_____

_____

Project name: _____

Who I'm making it for: _____

Occasion: _____

Start date: _____ End date: _____

Sketch

Notes:

_____

_____

_____

_____

_____

_____

_____

Yarn used

Color: _____

Dye lot: _____

Fiber: _____

Guage:_____

Weight: _____

WPI: _____

Hooks used:_____

Washing instructions:_____

_____

_____

Additional notes:

_____

_____

_____

_____

_____

_____

Project name: _____

Who I'm making it for: _____

Occasion: _____

Start date: _____ End date: _____

Sketch

Notes:

_____

_____

_____

_____

_____

_____

_____

Yarn used

Color: _____

Dye lot: _____

Fiber: _____

Guage: _____

Weight: _____

WPI: _____

Hooks used: _____

Washing instructions: _____

_____

_____

Additional notes:

_____

_____

_____

_____

_____

_____

Project name: _____

Who I'm making it for: _____

Occasion: _____

Start date: _____ End date: _____

Sketch

Notes:

_____

_____

_____

_____

_____

_____

_____

Yarn used

Color: _____

Dye lot: _____

Fiber: _____

Guage: _____

Weight: _____

WPI: _____

Hooks used: _____

Washing instructions: _____

_____

_____

Additional notes:

_____

_____

_____

_____

_____

_____

Project name: _____

Who I'm making it for: _____

Occasion: _____

Start date: _____ End date: _____

Sketch

Notes:

_____

_____

_____

_____

_____

_____

_____

Yarn used

Color: _____

Dye lot: _____

Fiber: _____

Guage: _____

Weight: _____

WPI: _____

Hooks used: _____

Washing instructions: _____

_____

_____

Additional notes:

_____

_____

_____

_____

_____

_____

Project name: _____

Who I'm making it for: _____

Occasion: _____

Start date: _____ End date: _____

Sketch

Notes:

_____

_____

_____

_____

_____

_____

_____

Yarn used

Color: _____

Dye lot: _____

Fiber: _____

Guage: _____

Weight: _____

WPI: _____

Hooks used: _____

Washing instructions: _____

_____

_____

Additional notes:

_____

_____

_____

_____

_____

_____

Project name: _____

Who I'm making it for: _____

Occasion: _____

Start date: _____ End date: _____

Sketch

Notes:

_____

_____

_____

_____

_____

_____

_____

Yarn used

Color: _____

Dye lot: _____

Fiber: _____

Guage: _____

Weight: _____

WPI: _____

Hooks used: _____

Washing instructions: _____

_____

_____

Additional notes:

_____

_____

_____

_____

_____

_____

Project name: _____

Who I'm making it for: _____

Occasion: _____

Start date: _____ End date: _____

Sketch

Notes:

_____

_____

_____

_____

_____

_____

_____

Yarn used

Color: _____

Dye lot: _____

Fiber: _____

Guage:_____

Weight: _____

WPI: _____

Hooks used:_____

Washing instructions:_____

_____

_____

Additional notes:

_____

_____

_____

_____

_____

_____

_____

Project name: _____

Who I'm making it for: _____

Occasion: _____

Start date: _____ End date: _____

Sketch

Notes:

_____

_____

_____

_____

_____

_____

_____

Yarn used

Color: _____

Dye lot: _____

Fiber: _____

Guage:_____

Weight: _____

WPI: _____

Hooks used:_____

Washing instructions:_____

_____

_____

Additional notes:

_____

_____

_____

_____

_____

_____

Project name: _____

Who I'm making it for: _____

Occasion: _____

Start date: _____ End date: _____

Sketch

Notes:

_____

_____

_____

_____

_____

_____

_____

Yarn used

Color: _____

Dye lot: _____

Fiber: _____

Guage: _____

Weight: _____

WPI: _____

Hooks used: _____

Washing instructions: _____

_____

_____

Additional notes:

_____

_____

_____

_____

_____

_____

Project name: _____

Who I'm making it for: _____

Occasion: _____

Start date: _____ End date: _____

Sketch

Notes:

_____

_____

_____

_____

_____

_____

Yarn used

Color: _____

Dye lot: _____

Fiber: _____

Guage: _____

Weight: _____

WPI: _____

Hooks used: _____

Washing instructions: _____

_____

_____

Additional notes:

_____

_____

_____

_____

_____

_____

Project name: _____

Who I'm making it for: _____

Occasion: _____

Start date: _____ End date: _____

Sketch

Notes:

_____

_____

_____

_____

_____

_____

_____

Yarn used

Color: _____

Dye lot: _____

Fiber: _____

Guage: _____

Weight: _____

WPI: _____

Hooks used: _____

Washing instructions: _____

_____

_____

Additional notes:

_____

_____

_____

_____

_____

_____

Project name: _____

Who I'm making it for: _____

Occasion: _____

Start date: _____ End date: _____

Sketch

Notes:

_____

_____

_____

_____

_____

_____

_____

Yarn used

Color: _____

Dye lot: _____

Fiber: _____

Guage:_____

Weight: _____

WPI: _____

Hooks used:_____

Washing instructions:_____

_____

_____

Additional notes:

_____

_____

_____

_____

_____

_____

Project name: _____

Who I'm making it for: _____

Occasion: _____

Start date: _____ End date: _____

Sketch

Notes:

_____

_____

_____

_____

_____

_____

Yarn used

Color: _____

Dye lot: _____

Fiber: _____

Guage: _____

Weight: _____

WPI: _____

Hooks used: _____

Washing instructions: _____

_____

_____

Additional notes:

_____

_____

_____

_____

_____

_____

Project name: _____

Who I'm making it for: _____

Occasion: _____

Start date: _____ End date: _____

Sketch

Notes:

_____

_____

_____

_____

_____

_____

_____

Yarn used

Color: _____

Dye lot: _____

Fiber: _____

Guage: _____

Weight: _____

WPI: _____

Hooks used: _____

Washing instructions: _____

_____

_____

Additional notes:

_____

_____

_____

_____

_____

_____

Project name: _____

Who I'm making it for: _____

Occasion: _____

Start date: _____ End date: _____

Sketch

Notes:

_____

_____

_____

_____

_____

_____

_____

Yarn used

Color: _____

Dye lot: _____

Fiber: _____

Guage: _____

Weight: _____

WPI: _____

Hooks used: _____

Washing instructions: _____

_____

_____

Additional notes:

_____

_____

_____

_____

_____

_____

Project name: _____

Who I'm making it for: _____

Occasion: _____

Start date: _____ End date: _____

Sketch

Notes:

_____

_____

_____

_____

_____

_____

_____

Yarn used

Color: _____

Dye lot: _____

Fiber: _____

Guage: _____

Weight: _____

WPI: _____

Hooks used: _____

Washing instructions: _____

_____

_____

Additional notes:

_____

_____

_____

_____

_____

_____

_____

Project name: _____

Who I'm making it for: _____

Occasion: _____

Start date: _____ End date: _____

Sketch

Notes:

_____

_____

_____

_____

_____

_____

Yarn used

Color: _____

Dye lot: _____

Fiber: _____

Guage:_____

Weight: _____

WPI: _____

Hooks used:_____

Washing instructions: _____

_____

_____

Additional notes:

_____

_____

_____

_____

_____

_____

Project name: _____

Who I'm making it for: _____

Occasion: _____

Start date: _____ End date: _____

Sketch

Notes:

_____

_____

_____

_____

_____

_____

_____

Yarn used

Color: _____

Dye lot: _____

Fiber: _____

Guage: _____

Weight: _____

WPI: _____

Hooks used: _____

Washing instructions: _____

_____

_____

Additional notes:

_____

_____

_____

_____

_____

_____

Project name: _____

Who I'm making it for: _____

Occasion: _____

Start date: _____ End date: _____

Sketch

Notes:

_____

_____

_____

_____

_____

_____

_____

Yarn used

Color: _____

Dye lot: _____

Fiber: _____

Guage: _____

Weight: _____

WPI: _____

Hooks used: _____

Washing instructions: _____

_____

_____

Additional notes:

_____

_____

_____

_____

_____

_____

Project name: _____

Who I'm making it for: _____

Occasion: _____

Start date: _____ End date: _____

Sketch

Notes:

_____
_____
_____
_____
_____
_____
_____

Yarn used

Color: _____

Dye lot: _____

Fiber: _____

Guage: _____

Weight: _____

WPI: _____

Hooks used: _____

Washing instructions: _____

_____

_____

Additional notes:

_____

_____

_____

_____

_____

_____

Project name: _____

Who I'm making it for: _____

Occasion: _____

Start date: _____ End date: _____

Sketch

Notes:

_____

_____

_____

_____

_____

_____

_____

Yarn used

Color: _____

Dye lot: _____

Fiber: _____

Guage: _____

Weight: _____

WPI: _____

Hooks used: _____

Washing instructions: _____

_____

_____

Additional notes:

_____

_____

_____

_____

_____

_____

Project name: _____

Who I'm making it for: _____

Occasion: _____

Start date: _____ End date: _____

Sketch

Notes:

_____

_____

_____

_____

_____

_____

_____

Yarn used

Color: _____

Dye lot: _____

Fiber: _____

Guage: _____

Weight: _____

WPI: _____

Hooks used: _____

Washing instructions: _____

_____

_____

Additional notes:

_____

_____

_____

_____

_____

_____

_____

Project name: _____

Who I'm making it for: _____

Occasion: _____

Start date: _____ End date: _____

Sketch

Notes:

_____

_____

_____

_____

_____

_____

_____

Yarn used

Color: _____

Dye lot: _____

Fiber: _____

Guage: _____

Weight: _____

WPI: _____

Hooks used: _____

Washing instructions: _____

_____

_____

Additional notes:

_____

_____

_____

_____

_____

_____

Project name: _____

Who I'm making it for: _____

Occasion: _____

Start date: _____ End date: _____

Sketch

Notes:

_____

_____

_____

_____

_____

_____

_____

Yarn used

Color: _____

Dye lot: _____

Fiber: _____

Guage: _____

Weight: _____

WPI: _____

Hooks used: _____

Washing instructions: _____

_____

_____

Additional notes:

_____

_____

_____

_____

_____

_____

Project name: _____

Who I'm making it for: _____

Occasion: _____

Start date: _____ End date: _____

Sketch

Notes:

_____

_____

_____

_____

_____

_____

_____

Yarn used

Color: _____

Dye lot: _____

Fiber: _____

Guage:_____

Weight: _____

WPI: _____

Hooks used:_____

Washing instructions:_____

_____

_____

Additional notes:

_____

_____

_____

_____

_____

_____

Project name: _____

Who I'm making it for: _____

Occasion: _____

Start date: _____ End date: _____

Sketch

Notes:

_____
_____
_____
_____
_____
_____
_____

Yarn used

Color: _____

Dye lot: _____

Fiber: _____

Guage: _____

Weight: _____

WPI: _____

Hooks used: _____

Washing instructions: _____

_____

_____

Additional notes:

_____

_____

_____

_____

_____

_____

Made in the USA
Middletown, DE
18 April 2023